3/5/14
33.00

grt 6

understanding mental health

Depression and Other Mood Disorders

JON EBEN FIELD

Crabtree Publishing Company
www.crabtreebooks.com

understanding mental health

Developed and produced by Plan B Book Packagers
www.planbbookpackagers.com
Author: Jon Eben Field
Editorial director: Ellen Rodger
Art director: Rosie Gowsell-Pattison
Project coordinator: Kathy Middleton
Editor: Molly Aloian
Proofreader: Wendy Scavuzzo
Production coordinator and prepress
    technician: Tammy McGarr
Print coordinator: Margaret Amy Salter

Library and Archives Canada Cataloguing in Publication

Field, Jon Eben, 1975-, author
        Depression and other mood disorders / Jon Eben Field.

(Understanding mental health)
Includes index.
Issued in print and electronic formats.
ISBN 978-0-7787-0084-5 (bound).--ISBN 978-0-7787-0090-6 (pbk.).--
ISBN 978-1-4271-9397-1 (pdf).--ISBN 978-1-4271-9391-9 (html)

        1. Depression, Mental--Juvenile literature. 2. Affective
disorders--Juvenile literature. I. Title.

RC537.F54 2014   j616.85'27   C2013-907571-2
                                            C2013-907572-0

Library of Congress Cataloging-in-Publication Data

CIP available at Library of Congress

Crabtree Publishing Company
www.crabtreebooks.com   1-800-387-7650

Printed in Canada/012014/BF20131120

Published in Canada
Crabtree Publishing
616 Welland Ave.
St. Catharines, ON
L2M 5V6

Published in the United States
Crabtree Publishing
PMB 59051
350 Fifth Avenue, 59th Floor
New York, New York 10118

Published in the United Kingdom
Crabtree Publishing
Maritime House
Basin Road North, Hove
BN41 1WR

Published in Australia
Crabtree Publishing
3 Charles Street
Coburg North
VIC, 3058

CONTENTS

Sometimes young people who are depressed don't have the typical symptoms. They may be irritable, angry, or even antisocial. This can make a diagnosis more difficult, particularly if this is thought to be normal.

The Dark Place

"It started slowly. After Malcolm and I split, I just felt a little sadder than usual. My friends kept saying, 'Get over it. You're better than him.' But it didn't matter. I started sleeping more, then I was cutting classes, then I would walk around the corner from my house and wait for my parents to go to work, then go back home and climb back in bed. I'd close my blinds and sleep. When I wasn't sleeping, I was crying. I was just drowning. It wasn't about Malcolm any more, either. It was everything. I felt really dark and empty. Nothing mattered. Especially me. My parents didn't get it. They told me that it was just a phase and I'd get over it. But I couldn't. I didn't know how. I stopped texting my friends. I just couldn't do anything. When it was really bad, it actually made me feel better to think I was dead because then, I wouldn't feel anything. When I texted 'goodbye' to my best friend, she called my mom. That's when I started to get help." — Vanessa, 16.

Let's Talk About Depression

Depression and mood disorders are common, but serious mental illnesses. Mood disorders affect the rich, poor, young, and old equally. They occur in people from all walks of life. Depression and other mood disorders are complex illnesses that affect the brains of sufferers and cause a variety of symptoms. When undiagnosed and untreated, these illnesses cause major upheavals in the sufferers' lives. They aren't just the blues—they are disorders that can lead to reckless or risk-taking behavior, **self-medication**, substance abuse, and attempted or successful suicide.

Many adolescents and teens suffer from depression and other mood disorders. They are among the most common mental health problems experienced by young people. They are generally caused by chemical imbalances in the brain. Some mood disorders are set off by environmental factors such as a lack of light during winter that can set up seasonal affective disorder. Often, depression and mood disorders are undiagnosed in adolescents and teens because the symptoms are dismissed as normal teenage "moodiness" or the "raging hormones" of puberty.

Depression is more than just moodiness. It's a serious condition that won't go away without treatment.

What Is Mental Illness?

Think you're going crazy? Afraid that you'll be shunned and made fun of if you seem "loopy" or **erratic**? That's not unusual for young people with depression or mood disorders. Mental health issues continue to be thought of as a dirty little secret that nobody is supposed to know or talk about. That's because people with a mental illness face significant **stigma**, or shame, and negative attitudes toward mental illness are prevalent. But a mental illness is nothing to be ashamed of. Mental illnesses are illnesses just like diabetes, asthma, or cancer. People do not choose to become mentally ill. They aren't faking it or doing it to be dark and mysterious. What's so dark and mysterious about hurting and feeling wretched?

When some people think of mental illness, they imagine a person muttering alone on a street corner. People with depression and mood disorders are doctors, writers, CEOs, teachers, politicians, and actors, including Angelina Jolie.

7

Depression can make you feel as though you are trapped in a fog or a bubble, with no apparent escape.

What Is Depression?

chapter 1

Depression is a mood disorder that makes a person feel so sad that they cannot function normally. Feeling depressed is more than just a "case of the blues." People feel sad as a normal part of life, and this should not be confused with depression. When someone is depressed, the type and level of their saddened mood is much greater than general sadness and occurs for a much longer period of time. It's normal to feel sad because of moving, your parents' divorce, the loss of a loved one, or breaking up with a girlfriend or boyfriend. Depression can happen as a result of stress or sadness but, at a certain point, the sadness experienced no longer "fits" what happened. Depression can also just happen for no apparent reason.

Depression affects approximately 14.8 million Americans a year (between 5 and 8 percent of the population). Doctors diagnose different types of depression based on the symptoms experienced and their severity. The term depression includes:

- Major depressive disorder
- Dysthymic disorder (chronic depression)
- Depression related to hormones (including postpartum depression, a type of depression that happens to women after they have given birth to a baby)

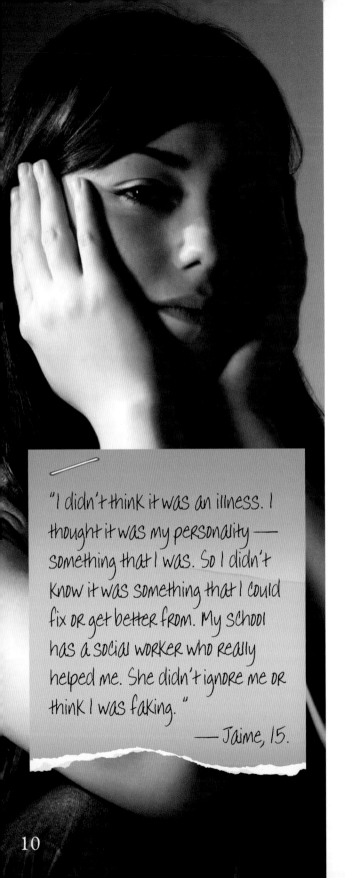

"I didn't think it was an illness. I thought it was my personality — something that I was. So I didn't know it was something that I could fix or get better from. My school has a social worker who really helped me. She didn't ignore me or think I was faking."

— Jaime, 15.

Why Depression?

Researchers who study depression and the brain believe there are a number of factors that increase a person's chance of becoming depressed. Research shows that depression is related to changes in brain chemistry where there is an imbalance of three **neurotransmitters** that affect mood–serotonin, norepinephrine, and dopamine. The imbalance prevents nerve cells in the brain (neurons) from communicating properly. Researchers believe there is a genetic basis to this chemical imbalance as depression is more prevalent in people who have relatives diagnosed with the illness. Scientists are searching for the "depression genes." It is also important to remember that people with no history of depression in their families can be diagnosed too.

Symptoms of Depression

You've probably heard a friend say "I'm so depressed" to describe how they feel sad or bummed out about something. With so many people using the term to describe temporary unhappiness, the real signs and symptoms of depression can be dismissed or ignored. But doctors and **psychologists** measure depression differently. People who report four or more of these symptoms should see their doctor:

- Frequently feeling sad without a reason
- Little to no pleasure doing things that were ordinarily enjoyed
- Feeling numb inside
- Sleeping all the time and struggling to get out of bed
- Feeling angry, frustrated, or annoyed very easily
- Feeling anxious all the time
- Difficulty concentrating and frequently forgetting simple things
- Frequent thoughts about death and/or suicide (called suicide ideation)
- Feeling hopeless, worthless, or guilty
- Gaining or losing a lot of weight
- Feeling fatigued and without energy
- Overeating or loss of appetite
- More frequent alcohol or drug use
- Difficulty making decisions

Eating mindlessly may be one of many signs of depression.

Major Depressive Disorder

Major depressive disorder is the most common form of depression and severely affects the lives of people suffering from it. It is characterized by a very low mood and a condition called anhedonia (a lack of interest in pleasure or things that were ordinarily enjoyed). The change in mood must last for at least two weeks and impair a person's ability to function normally. Women and girls are twice as likely as men and boys to experience major depression. The symptoms of major depressive disorder vary from person to person, but they almost always include intense despair. People suffering from major depressive disorder lack energy, experience a loss of appetite, struggle to concentrate, feel debilitating sadness, and have frequent suicidal thoughts. Some people may only have one major depressive episode in their lives. Others have several. One study showed that if a high school has 1,000 students, within one year, 77 students will likely suffer from major depression.

Dysthymic Disorder

Dysthymic disorder, also called chronic depression, is similar to major depressive disorder except that symptoms are not usually as severe. Also, dysthymic disorder lasts for a much longer time. This form of depression is diagnosed after someone has had symptoms of low mood for a period of two years for adults, or one year for children and adolescents. People who suffer from dysthymic disorder frequently do not seek out treatment, because they see their symptoms as part of their personality. They may act withdrawn, quiet, and gloomy, but sufferers often see these expressions of the disorder as part of who they are.

People often describe
major depression as
feeling that "nothing
matters," "it's impossible
to get out of bed," or
"I hate myself and I'm
totally worthless."

13

Hormone-Related Disorders

Sometimes, the hormones in our bodies get out of whack and this can lead to serious depression-like symptoms. Depression related to hormones includes premenstrual dysphoric disorder (PMDD) and postpartum depression, both of which are experienced exclusively by women. PMDD is a severe form of premenstrual syndrome that includes intense mood and physical symptoms each month that are more severe and disruptive than premenstrual syndrome. Symptoms include extreme irritability, feeling anxious, mood swings, and crying, as well as changes in sleep, appetite, and ability to concentrate. Evidence shows that the same neurotransmitters that play a part in depression, affect mood changes in PMDD.

Postpartum depression is experienced as feelings of great sadness during the six months following the birth of a child. One in ten new mothers have postpartum depression. It can be difficult for teen moms who may have less support from family. Stress can make postpartum depression and PMDD symptoms worse.

Hormone-related depression is real, but not everybody who is moody and crampy has PMDD.

You're Not Alone

About 20 percent of teenagers develop depression and many will suffer symptoms for eight months to a year before getting help. Statistically, girls seem to suffer more from depression, but boys are less likely to seek help. The good news is that it doesn't have to be this way. There is help available and there are many effective treatments.

Thoughts that race as fast as a speeding train are common with some mood disorders such as bipolar disorder.

Chapter 2

Other Mood Disorders

Ever feel as though you are on an emotional roller coaster, reaching unbelievable heights of energy and happiness for a time, and then falling into horrible crashing lows? People with mood disorders such as bipolar disorder, have periods of extreme highs followed by deep lows. Bipolar disorder is one of many mood disorders, or depressive disorders, that can be very difficult to diagnose in adolescents and teenagers.

Mood disorders are complex illnesses. Researchers don't know their exact cause but they believe they are influenced by genetic, biochemical, and environmental factors. Like depression, it is thought that imbalances in the brain's neurotransmitters cause mood disorders. Depression is a feature of many mood disorders. Mood disorders include:

- Bipolar Disorder
- Cyclothymic Disorder
- Seasonal Affective Disorder (SAD)

These mood disorders are also equal opportunity illnesses. They effect people of all races, ages, and genders.

Bipolar Disorder

Bipolar disorder used to be called manic-depressive disorder. It is characterized by a cycle of high and low moods. What this means is that people with bipolar disorder experience periods of mania where they have intense energy, feel like they don't need to sleep, and have a whirlwind of thoughts going through their heads. This period of euphoria, or extreme happiness, is followed by periods of deep depression called a "depressive phase." In a manic state, bipolar disorder sufferers may lose touch with reality as their thoughts become too fast and they try to accomplish too much. In the subsequent depressed phase, they feel as though they have no energy and cannot do anything at all. People who are bipolar often spend many years going from the peaks of mania to the valleys of depression and back again, without getting proper treatment.

About 250 million people around the world are bipolar. The disorder usually surfaces between the ages of 16–25, but can also occur much earlier or later. Many children and youths diagnosed as bipolar also have a **comorbidity**, or another disorder occurring at the same time, such as attention deficit hyperactivity disorder (ADHD).

Not just a face in the crowd? Mood disorders are fairly common.

Types of Bipolar Disorder

There are two major types of bipolar disorder. Bipolar I disorder is the most common form of the illness. People diagnosed with bipolar 1 disorder often have deeper depressive phases that make it difficult for them to function. Bipolar II disorder is similar to bipolar I disorder, except that the experience of mania is less severe. This type of mania is called hypomania. The cycle of high and low moods are a natural part of this illness and, unless treated, will make life difficult.

Mood cycles vary for someone who is bipolar. If someone has four or more episodes of mania and depression during a year, then that person suffers from rapid cycling. Approximately 15 percent of people who are bipolar experience rapid cycling in the course of their illness. The period of a cycle may last several months, while some may experience depression in the morning and mania in the evening.

During acute mania, some people with bipolar disorder may spend too much money, consume too much alcohol, and behave recklessly.

Cyclothymic Disorder

Cyclothymic disorder is a subcategory of bipolar disorder that is characterized by less severe mood swings. Many patients with cyclothymic disorder go for long periods without diagnosis or treatment because the range of their mood cycle is less pronounced than bipolar disorder. Often during the hypomanic phase of this disorder, the patient will experience irritability rather than euphoria.

People with cyclothymic disorder have a 50 percent chance of developing either bipolar I disorder or bipolar II disorder. In fact, many cyclothymic patients are only diagnosed after they have progressed into a form of bipolar disorder. Because of this, people with cyclothymic disorder may experience many years of mood swings as a young person and adult before getting treatment.

"I always knew I was a little different than other people as a kid. I just didn't know why that was. I had to go through a lot of suffering before I was diagnosed, and my behavior was wild. Even after, it took a while to figure out what treatment worked for me. Now I know this is normal and this is me. I have a disorder but the disorder does not have me."

— Annetta, adult with bipolar disorder.

Not Just "The Winter Blues"

Ever notice how gloomy some people get when it is rainy outside and how their spirits lift when the sun is out? Now imagine this 100 times worse. The long, dark winters in the **northern hemisphere** can lead to a condition called Seasonal Affective Disorder, which is a winter depression. Researchers believe the lack of sunlight can affect brain chemicals in some people, leading to the depression. Although SAD sufferers are not suffering from true depression, they experience symptoms similar to depression which can be treated with light therapy (use of a special light) and medication for depression. Studies have also shown that northern populations in places such as Alaska or Canada have a statistically higher occurrence of SAD.

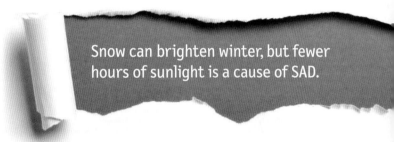

Snow can brighten winter, but fewer hours of sunlight is a cause of SAD.

Just because depression seems to have always been there, doesn't mean it shouldn't be treated. Depression isn't a choice. It is an illness that can be treated.

Chapter 3

Diagnosis and Treatment

When dealing with depression and mood disorders, seeking help is the first step toward becoming healthy and managing your life. There are many different health care professionals who can assist you in becoming well again. You may seek out a doctor or **psychiatrist**, psychologist, psychotherapist, social worker, counselor, or other health care professional. Before offering a diagnosis, a health care professional will consider the range of symptoms you have been experiencing.

The most current diagnostic tool used by many psychiatrists and health care professionals is the American Psychiatric Association's *Diagnostic and Statistical Manual of Mental Disorders* (DSM). By listening carefully to patients and observing their behavior, mental health professionals can determine the underlying symptoms of a mental illness and provide a diagnosis.

Talking with a health care professional about your moods and emotional pain can be difficult, but not impossible.

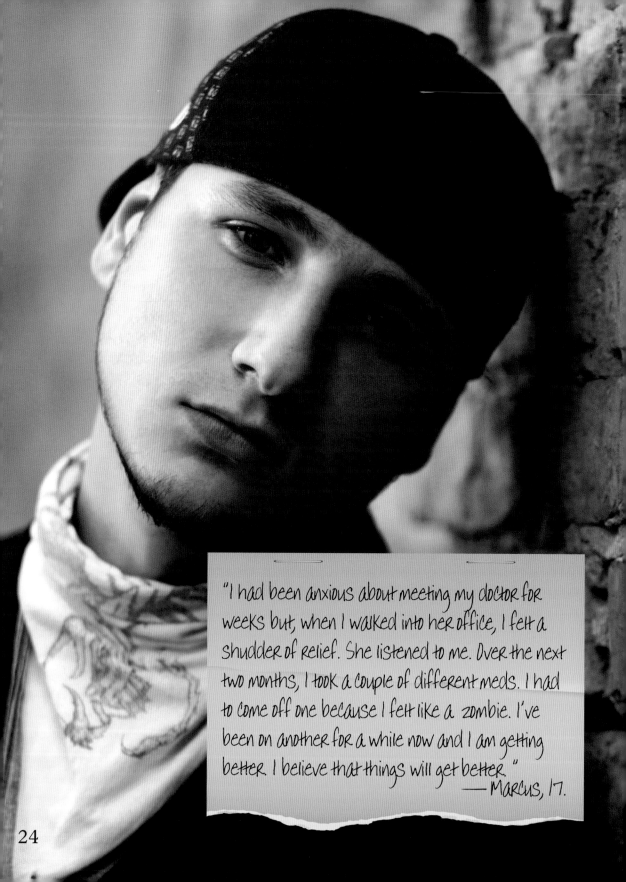

"I had been anxious about meeting my doctor for weeks but, when I walked into her office, I felt a shudder of relief. She listened to me. Over the next two months, I took a couple of different meds. I had to come off one because I felt like a zombie. I've been on another for a while now and I am getting better. I believe that things will get better."
—Marcus, 17.

24

Diagnosis isn't foolproof—sometimes doctors give an incorrect opinion. For example, young children with bipolar disorder are frequently **misdiagnosed** as having ADHD. People with bipolar disorder sometimes have to see many different doctors or psychiatrists before being properly diagnosed. Like other medical conditions, mood disorders can be diagnosed because they have a set of symptoms that generally appear across the illness. The key to proper treatment is having a correct diagnosis. Mood disorders are not a result of a personal failing or lack of character. They are based in biology, genetics, and environmental stressors. We would not criticize or think less of someone who has diabetes, so we should treat people with mood disorders no differently.

The Many Steps of Treatment

In North America, the first line of treatment for depression and mood disorders is often medication in combination with counseling, or talk therapy. The types of medication used include **antidepressants**, mood stabilizers, and anti-anxiety pills. How a person experiences their illness will determine the medication used to treat it. These medications typically affect how your brain sends and receives messages.

As people become depressed, or cycle between highs and lows as they do with bipolar disorder, their normal living patterns lose consistency. Because these illnesses disrupt appetite and sleep patterns, a key part of any healthy recovery involves a regular sleeping and eating schedule. Eating healthy meals at a regular time, and keeping a consistent sleeping and waking schedule, are essential to maintaining a regular circadian rhythm, or daily pattern of waking, sleeping, and living. This regular cycle will help people with depression and mood disorders be more aware of variations in their moods that are outside

Drugs and Research

One of the most significant advances in the treatment of depression was the development of the first antidepressants in the 1950s. These chemically derived medications were monoamine oxidase inhibitors (MAOIs) and were the first drugs to relieve the symptoms of depression. Unfortunately, many MAOIs interacted with chemicals found in foods such as sausages, beer, wine, cheese, and avocados, causing very serious side effects that made their continued use impossible for patients. Around the same time, another family of early antidepressants was discovered: the tricyclics. Some people experienced severe side effects from these drugs as well, and tricyclics were often fatal in overdose.

Brain Chemical Imbalances

As scientists continued to study depression, they came to believe that depression and other mood disorders were a result of chemical imbalances in the brain. There were three neurotransmitters that affected these disorders: serotonin, dopamine, and norepinephrine. Serotonin influences mood generally. Dopamine affects our focus, motivation, and pleasure. Norepinephrine affects our levels of wakefulness and general energy. Most scientists believe that imbalances in these neurotransmitters are a root cause in a range of mood disorders.

Medications work on correcting imbalances in brain chemistry. Counseling helps patients understand their behavior and emotions.

SSRI Drugs

The next group of medications was designed to address the specific imbalances of neurotransmitters. The most widely used medications are the selective serotonin reuptake inhibitors (SSRIs). In the brain, messages are passed between nerve cells. These medications work by allowing the brain's circuits and nerve cells to communicate and pass on information more effectively. The most famous SSRI is fluoxetine or, as it is better known, Prozac. Paxil, Zoloft, and Celexa are the brand names of several other SSRIs commonly used to treat depression and other mood disorders.

SSRIs and Teens

The use of SSRIs for adolescents and teens is controversial because some of these medications have not been approved for people in this age group. As well, studies have shown that teens have an increased risk of suicidal ideation, or thinking about suicide, when they first start taking many antidepressants. Because of these links, doctors will usually more closely monitor teens who are taking SSRIs. SSRIs can be very effective in easing depression. Abruptly stopping SSRIs can lead to serious physical and mental pain and problems thinking clearly.

Headaches, sweating, dry mouth, and nausea are possible side effects from SSRIs.

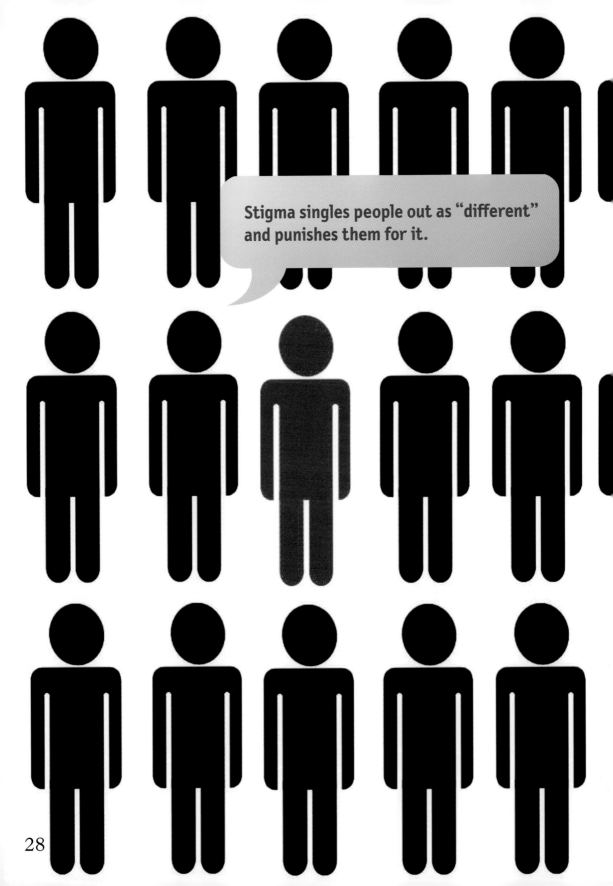

Stigma singles people out as "different" and punishes them for it.

28

Chapter 4
Dealing With Stigma

When you imagine someone having a mental illness such as depression or bipolar disorder, what do you see? Many people picture a homeless person standing on a street corner making gestures in the air while carrying on a conversation with themselves. Others see people who choose not to work, get out of bed, or leave the house because they lack willpower or a strong character. Others imagine people who suffer unfulfilled lives and they feel sympathy for them, but are quick to point out that they have never known anyone with these illnesses.

Stigma is an unfortunate side effect of centuries of the fear and misunderstanding of mood disorders. Stigma is a negative **stereotype**. The term comes from ancient Greece where it meant to "mark or tattoo." At that time, stigma was marked on slaves and undesirables, or people whose presence was not wanted. In many ways, people suffering from mood disorders experience similar **ostracism** because of misunderstandings about what the illnesses are. People with cancer are not stigmatized because of their illness, yet people with mood disorders experience multiple forms of **discrimination** daily.

Stigma Hurts

Being stigmatized is horrible. The level of discrimination toward the mentally ill is very high in our society and can make life difficult. People with mood disorders are frequently ostracized as lower-class citizens because the origins of their illness are not properly understood. Imagine trying to manage a mood disorder while people make fun of you, don't want to be around you, or think you are stupid and unable to understand anything. Stigma makes the illness worse because it contributes to feelings of worthlessness.

"When I was in high school, I was the kid in dark clothes who skulked around corners. My parents didn't care what I did. I was a castaway and all the different cliques of kids looked down on me. I didn't know it then, but I was suffering from depression. Ten years later, I recognize that the bullying, exclusion, and physical and emotional abuse that was a regular part of my life was not about me. I was discriminated against because of fear."

— Weston, adult with depression.

Fear and Loathing

Many talented, intelligent, and successful people live with depression and mood disorders, but they feel they cannot speak openly of their condition because of the stigma attached to their illness. When they do, there is always that underlying sense of judgment. But mood disorder success stories are what is required to dispel the myths and negative stereotypes about mental illness. Keeping things hidden only contributes to centuries-old superstitions, assumptions, and misinformation.

The social world of adolescence is a difficult one to travel at the best of times. When someone is suffering from depression or bipolar disorder, their ability to handle peer groups and social pressure is weakened. People with mood disorders do not choose to feel or act as they do, and often they do not know what to do to turn their situation round. People sometimes turn to alcohol or drugs to deal with stress, which makes things worse.

Singer and actress Demi Lovato spoke out about being diagnosed with bipolar disorder after treatment for substance abuse. She has said she battled depression from a young age and, since her diagnosis, has felt it was important to help young people fight stigma.

31

Are You Part of the Problem?

Have you ever felt alone and powerless? That's how people with mental health disorders sometimes feel. Now imagine feeling that way and having to deal with the negative stereotypes of misinformed people. The only way to effectively fight stigma is to counter the stupid with the smart. Stigma can be fought with information, understanding, and communication. Nasty behavior toward people with a mental illness is unacceptable. To begin to fight against stigma, you must ask whether you use language, watch films or media representations, or make jokes about mental illness that portray mentally ill people negatively. Perhaps you like to say to a friend, "you're crazy!" about a strange or weird statement they've made, or "don't act so schizo!" Both of these statements demean the mentally ill.

Seriously? Would you feel good about spreading gossip about a person's mental health?

How You Can Stop the Stigma

Stigma is the prejudice and stereotyping of people. To stop it from happening to people who have a mental illness or mental health disorder you need to know fact from myth. Your attitude and actions can make a difference in people's lives.

1. Be aware of the facts. Experts believe up to 70 percent of adult mental illness begins during childhood or adolescence.

2. Mental health disorders often have many causes but the main causes, as with all illnesses, are biological and environmental. A person who has a mental health issue is not at fault. Neither they, nor their parents caused the illness.

3. Recognize that your discriminatory behavior plays a part in stigma. Discrimination is unjust as is prejudicial treatment of others because of who they are. Make an effort to change how you act and what you say to people. Why act like a jerk just for fun?

4. What you say and how you act are important. Calling people names, spreading gossip, or being otherwise hurtful is just plain mean. Just like other slurs, calling people "crazy" or "nuts" is inappropriate, nasty, and rude.

5. Treat people with a mental health problem the way you would like to be treated. Support your classmates, friends, or family members.

6. Educate yourself and keep a positive attitude. If you find people spreading myths, give them the facts.

Positive self-talk can actually help erase fear and other self-defeating thoughts. It is one method of managing moods and behaviors.

Chapter 5

Managing Moods

If you have been diagnosed with a mood disorder, your life will change. How it changes is based partly on what you do to adapt to your new reality. One very important aspect of dealing with a mood disorder is learning to manage your moods. There are a number of techniques that can have positive effects on your daily life, and there are other choices that can have negative effects.

Both alcohol and drugs are frequently used by people with mood disorders as a form of self-medication. In cases where this happens, the sufferer will use either alcohol or drugs to manage their mood swings and try to level themselves out. The major problems with this are that drugs and alcohol can make the symptoms of mood disorders much worse, and also cause addiction. People who suffer from a mental illness along with drug or alcohol addiction are given what is called a dual diagnosis. This indicates that they suffer from a mental illness and a comorbid substance-abuse problem.

Self-medication can lead to addiction. Research shows many people with addictions have undiagnosed mental health issues.

Banish Negative Self-talk

What happens if the voice in your head tells you that you are stupid and worthless? Many people with depression and other mood disorders engage in negative self-talk. It's not a crazy voice, it's your self-esteem breaking down with negative thinking. Studies have shown that positive self-talk, even when you don't feel particularly positive, can help to change your mood for the better. Positive self-talk is a feedback loop. When we say positive things about ourselves, we feel better, which makes it easier to say positive things. Establishing this pattern can be hard, but it is ultimately a very powerful tool for changing your attitude toward life. Here are some tips for positive self-talk:

1. I have a very common illness and I am getting help. There are people I trust and people who love me who can help me when I feel that things are out of control.

2. I am an important person. I have talents and skills that nobody else has.

3. I can help myself by recognizing my mood swings or when I am starting to feel down.

4. What other people think of me is not important. I know that I am a good person. I am not afraid to be myself.

Suicidal Thoughts

Thinking about ending it all–or what doctors and counselors call suicidal ideation–is very real for adolescents and teens dealing with depression and mood disorders. Suicide rates are higher among people with mental health disorders. Young males are also at a much higher risk of suicide than young females. You need to know that thinking about suicide is common. You are not alone in this, so sharing your thoughts of suicide with someone can help you not act on your thoughts. You won't always feel bad, even though it's hard to believe that when you feel miserable and worthless. Things can and do get better. If you can't talk to someone you know, call a suicide hotline (see the numbers in the Other Resources section of this book).

"I've been there. You are not alone. There are people who care and you can find help. Being diagnosed with a mood disorder is not a life sentence. It is possible to successfully navigate life and thrive. I should know. I wrote this book and I have bipolar disorder."
— Jon Eben, adult with bipolar disorder

Fighting Fear: Within and Without

Sometimes, dealing with depression or a mood disorder might feel as though you are drawn into a whirlpool of negativity. Although medication and therapy are essential to recovery, there are a number of techniques you can use on your own. Guided meditation, relaxation exercises, and visualizations are all proven methods to help banish negative thoughts.

Guided meditation or relaxation exercises are frequently available as CDs, as well as online downloads. There is usually relaxing music played while a script is read. The script may sound a little funny at first but, if you focus on the words, it can help calm your mind. Here is an example of a guided meditation script:

Imagine that you have been transported to a tropical island. As you lie comfortably on the beach, you feel the sun gently warming your skin as a refreshing breeze ripples the ocean waves. The gentle rush of water up the beach is met with the faint sound of music in the air in the distance. You feel your body relax deeply as this tropical paradise causes you to become more at ease. You enjoy happy thoughts as the air around you sparkles with calm and peace. With each breath in, you relax into the smells and feelings of this perfect space. With each breath out, you release any residual tension or pain. Your entire body is calm and filled with a sense of golden light....

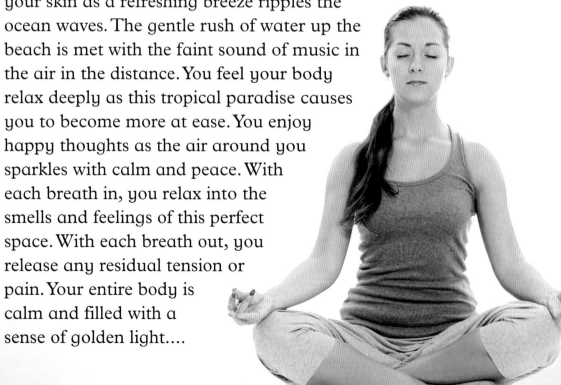

Emotional Overload

Sadly, feelings of anger and frustration are daily experiences for people suffering with depression or bipolar disorder. You may feel mad at yourself or you may blame others for the lack of connection you feel with the world. But regardless of the set of triggers that cause anger and frustration, learning to recognize them is the first step toward breaking this cycle.

For people with mood disorders, it is frequently very difficult to separate the emotions that come from within from emotions that come from how others treat them. A large part of gaining insight into anger, and learning to defuse its power, is recognizing when it emerges. If a certain person, situation, or topic makes you feel angry or frustrated, it may be worthwhile to avoid that trigger until you feel stronger. If that is not possible, then analyzing the situation to discover why it bothers you will help you make better decisions in relation to your emotions.

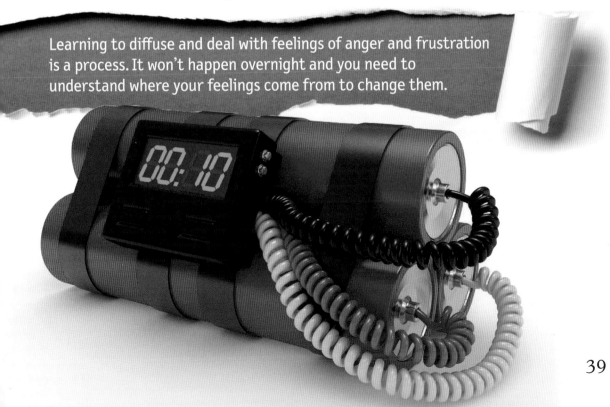

Learning to diffuse and deal with feelings of anger and frustration is a process. It won't happen overnight and you need to understand where your feelings come from to change them.

Having supportive family or friends can help with recovery, but the people who support you need support too.

Chapter 6
Family and Friends

You may have noticed that someone you care about (a friend, sibling, parent, or other relation) has started acting differently. You may find yourself saying things like, "They just don't seem the same," or "I don't remember them acting this way before," or "I feel like I don't know them anymore." Some change in people over the course of a life of experience is normal, but when those changes amount to something much larger, you may wonder what you can do to help. You may want to seek out a school counselor, teacher, or other trusted adult to discuss your concerns about a person's behavior and attitude shifts.

The first and most important thing to remember is that your loved one is still there. Depression and mood disorders affect how a person behaves, and may even cause them to act in ways that are out of character. They may do something that is hurtful to you or seem unresponsive to your desire to help. Try not to take these things personally. Living with and through a mood disorder frequently causes people to lose perspective on their life and what is important within it.

It's pretty hard to hide feelings of depression.

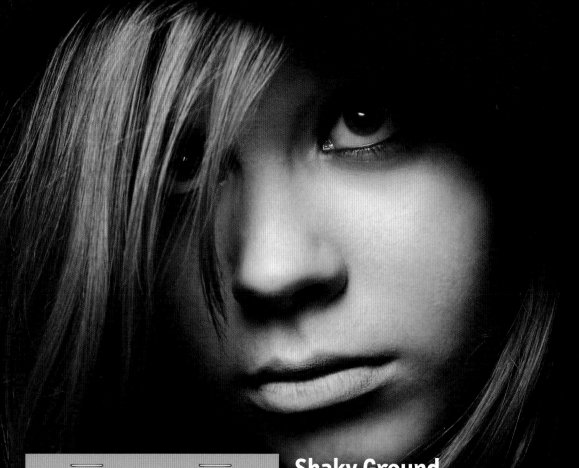

"My mom can be all calm one moment, then she freaks out on me and she'll cry and slam doors. My friends say their parents do this too, but not like this. Sometimes I can't even talk to her, she's so spun out. I hate that she's like this. I love her, but I hate her moods. I never know what to expect."

— Claire, 16.

Shaky Ground

If someone in your family develops depression or a mood disorder, there will be changes in your household. The person with the illness is dealing with confusion and change. Mental disorders can be very destructive to relationships. Sometimes, people with depression will even attempt to sever relationships to prevent themselves from taking you down with them. A major priority is making sure that your needs are met. Without your primary needs met, it is nearly impossible to provide support for others.

Caregiver Support

Taking care of and dealing with someone with depression or a mood disorder can take a lot of time and energy. Here are some quick tips for relieving stress in daily life:

- Get and use a stress ball
- Practice stretches
- Do yoga
- Go for a short walk or jog
- Take dance lessons
- Play a sport

These quick activities can help you deal with stress by exercising your body or getting you into a different environment. Caring for a friend or family member can seem to be a big burden, but there are numerous organizations that provide support both for the mentally ill and their families. It's very helpful to have a group of people you can speak to about your experiences living with someone with a mood disorder. This provides a space to vent your anger and air frustration without taking it out on your loved one. Also, it is very important to remember that sometimes a home environment is not the best place for someone who is deeply depressed or experiencing severe mood swings. Psychiatric hospitals provide essential emergency care in those situations when family members engage in behavior that places themselves or others at risk. There is nothing shameful in entering a psychiatric ward for assistance. For many people, doing so has been the lifeline that has kept them and their families on their feet.

Chapter 7

Depression Toolbox

Mood disorders such as depression and bipolar disorder, unfortunately, do not miraculously disappear. For many people, the struggle occurs over months or years and, for others, the struggle lasts their entire lives. Nonetheless, there are many ways to live a fulfilling life with the diagnosis of a mood disorder.

Coping With Challenges

There are ways to cope with the daily challenges. Being prepared and understanding your limits can help a lot when you are in difficult social situations that might make you feel fearful or not good enough. It's also important to never give up. Life can be a struggle sometimes, but it can get better.

Pack Your Box

There are a number of helpful tools to assist you in your daily experience with mental illness.

- Don't sweat the small stuff. Although this saying seems simplistic, it is very helpful when trying to focus on what really matters in life. You may feel as though you are drowning, that nothing matters, and there is little point, but the reality is that life is precious. You can make it through this day and find meaning.

- In your wallet or purse, keep a card with a list of important names and numbers. Your parents, friends, doctor, therapist, helpline, or someone you trust should be on the list. When you are in a difficult spot, have these numbers handy so you can simply call. When making this card, alert the people on this list that they may one day receive a call.

- Be generous with yourself. Everyone has good days and bad days. It is important to take care of yourself by remembering that you are just one person.

- Know that seeking help is not a sign of weakness. Knowing when to ask for help is a sign of inner strength and wisdom. If you feel as though you cannot cope, seek out help. If you have a good relationship with your parents, speak to them. If you have a teacher, friend, counselor, doctor, or coach that you trust, speak with them. If you ask someone for help, but they don't know where you should go, ask other people until you find the help you need.

Other Resources

There are a number of helpful books and websites that you can consult for further information about depression and other mood disorders. These resources are aimed primarily at adolescents, but also have a wide range of helpful information for anyone seeking to understand mood disorders better.

Helpful Hotlines
National Alliance on Mental Illness
1-800-950-6264
This is a toll-free (U.S.) 10 a.m. to 6 p.m. (EST) national hotline staffed with trained volunteers who can supply information and support for anyone (adolescents, teens, friends, parents) with questions about mental illness.

National Suicide Hotline
1-800-SUICIDE (784-2433)
This toll-free 24-hour national service connects you to a trained counselor at a nearby suicide crisis center. The service is confidential.

National Suicide Prevention Lifeline
1-800-273-8255
A free, confidential, hotline. Excellent articles and resources can be found at their website: www.suicidepreventionlifeline.org

Websites
CopeCareDeal
www.copecaredeal.org

CopeCareDeal is a website aimed at a teen audience that deals with mental illness and mood disorders. Along with helpful articles on suicide, bipolar disorder, and depression, there is a helpful and extensive glossary of terms and a list of other recommended online resources.

Mind Your Mind
mindyourmind.ca

An informational teen-oriented mental health site with information on how to get help, as well as personal stories about coping, struggles, and successes, a blog, and interactive tools that can help you identify and cope with your mental health disorder.

Teens Health
kidshealth.org

A safe information source on all aspects of teen health, including mental health. Available in English or Spanish.

Black Dog Institute
www.blackdoginstitute.org.au

This Australian-based institute's website contains excellent articles, videos for teens on bipolar disorder, depression, and other mood disorders, information on self-care, and questionnaires.

Teen Mental Health
teenmentalhealth.org

A useful website on a number of mental health topics for youths, their families, and teachers. The site focuses on evidence-based medicine, with trustworthy research articles.

Glossary

antidepressants Drugs that make depression less severe

comorbidity A disorder that happens at the same time as another disorder

discrimination Unjust treatment of different people on the grounds of race, gender, age, or ability

erratic Something that is unpredictable or uneven, such as behavior

misdiagnosed To make an incorrect diagnosis of a disease or illness

neurotransmitters Chemicals that help the brain function and transfer impulses

northern hemisphere The half of Earth that is north of the equator

ostracism The exclusion of someone or some group of people from society

psychiatrist A doctor with specialized training in diagnosing and treating mental illness and disorders of the brain

psychologists Experts or specialists in the study of mental and emotional problems

self-medication To use street drugs and alcohol to not feel emotional or physical pain

stereotype An oversimplified and incorrect view or idea about a person or group of people

stigma Unwarranted shame associated with a specific disorder or illness

Index